"

Every moment is an organizing opportunity, every person a potential activist, every minute a chance to change the world.

Dolores Huerta

Design by Yoke
www.thisisyoke.com
Typeset in Freight Sans Pro
First printing 2019
Photo credits:
p1 - ACORN
p31-32 - Sneinton Alchemy CIC

Community Organisers
www.corganisers.org.uk
@corganisers
facebook.com/corganisers
hello@corganisers.org.uk
(+44) 01985 213387
(+44) 07591 206913

Contributing writers and editors:
Nick Gardham & Marilyn Taylor

Contributing ideas and experience:
Helen Wallis-Dowling & the Community Organisers trainer network

10 Silver Street, Warminster, Wiltshire BA12 8PS
Community Organisers Ltd is a Company Limited by Guarantee registered in England and Wales with the company number 08180454.
Registered charity number 1183487

ISBN - 978-1-9163190-0-4

CONTENTS

Forewords 1

Supporting statements 5

Introduction 9

What community organising is 10

The community organising framework 11

Principles of practice 25

Different approaches to community 33
organising

How community organising relates 37
to other forms of empowerment and
social action

Forms of Engagement 39
Development and Dialogue 45
Action 57
Organisational Development 65
Public Service Approaches 71

What are the main similarities between 83
community organising and other
approaches

How to recognise community 85
organising

References 87

Last words 89

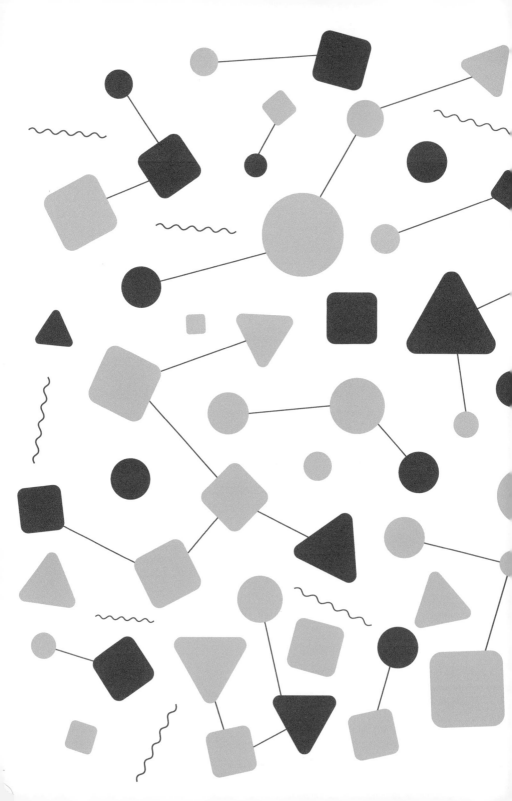

FOREWORD

Firstly, I would like to thank the staff of Community Organisers, for crafting this piece of work which for people who are looking to explore differing ways of working within communities should be a source of real insight.

At a time where the truth appears to be an elastic concept and appropriation of approaches can be used to subvert its original intention, I believe that to define what community organising is, and equally importantly, what it isn't, is really valuable and timely. When those in positions of power are seeking to use techniques to retain the status quo, it's important for us to be transparent about why we do what we do and how we do it.

And it couldn't be more important. As the United Kingdom embarks on the next phase of its journey following its departure form the EU, there is now a real and genuine pressing need for those of us in our sector, not only to stand up and be heard, but to shut up and listen. Building the peace in our fractured country, with hurting citizens, is going to become one of the most important roles for a generation. I hope, for all our sakes, that this book can help shape, explain and demonstrate some of the ways in which this can be done.

Sacha Bedding

Chair – Board of Trustees
Community Organisers

FOREWORD

For three years Community Organisers have been developing an approach to training people in the tools and principles of grass-roots community organising. We have trained over 3,500 people in community organising across England; people from all backgrounds and types of experience, from those with lived experience of the issues they are trying to change, to those in paid professional roles trying to change the way they work to incorporate a community organising approach into their frontline work with people and communities.

Along the way, there have been many fascinating discussions about what community organising is and what it isn't.

We have now reached the point where we felt it would be helpful to publish something which sets out our take on this question.

How does community organising differ from the huge range of methods and approaches to developing community, strengthening democracy and fighting for social justice which are available to all of us who want to achieve change?

How would we decide which approach to choose? Why do we think that community organising has a distinctive role to play? What is different about it and how would you know if you met a community organiser, rather than an activist, a politician or a community connector?

This is our interpretation, and we take full responsibility for any mistakes we may have made in describing any method or activity. Everything in this book is our own opinion as to differences and similarities. We hope it helps to bring some clarity about language and approaches.

We welcome dialogue and debate about this – so please let us have your views on this book by contacting us here:

https://www.corganisers.org.uk/contact-us/

N Gardham

Nick Gardham
Chief Executive

D. Diamond

Naomi Diamond
Programme Manager

SUPPORTING STATEMENTS

"

I'm really excited about this! Community organising isn't a new concept, it is something that many people do naturally if they care about their community. There is, however, a subtle difference between community organising and other practices, and it is great to have something that describes that difference and why we think that our work is especially important.

Dot Kirk-Adams - Experienced Community Organiser,
Let's Co-organise, Brighton

"

From the 1850s' trade unionists have played an important role in determining and defining the narrative around community organising. Community organising is not something that happens in isolation, it begins through developing authentic relationships, where conversations up-skill, empower, motivate and mobilise. This publication is a useful tool for all activists, to continue the debate around the principles of community organising and identifying the practices that make community organising unique and effective.

Bianca Todd - Founder Ron Todd Foundation

"

This is an extremely useful publication, which demystifies different approaches to citizenship and participation. It's very helpful when making decisions about how best to invest resources to get the best outcomes. Poor health and wellbeing is associated with a lack of control over your circumstances. Community organising demonstrates a way to give people back this control and addresses issues of inequality and lack of power in a positive way.

Anna Hartley FFPH - Director Public Health, Wakefield Council

"

Community organising offers a practical, effective (and energising!) way for communities to work together to tackle issues of social injustice. It's a way to build power, to develop long term, public relationships and to hold decision makers- and ourselves- to account. This guide sets out the breadth and variety of approaches communities can use in responding to the issues affecting them, and outlines the distinct role community organising has in doing so.

Kay Polley and Sam Rex-Edwards - lead organisers, TCC (Trefnu Cymunedol Cymru / Together Creating Communities)

"

This book is a timely analysis of the many different ways in which people come together to tackle social injustices and make a difference in their communities. This book sets out, clearly and accessibly, ways in which community organisers, public sector workers, activists, civil servants, and others can build the power of people using the tools most appropriate to the circumstances. I am proud to have worked with Community Organisers over a number of years and have seen first-hand the impact that grassroots organising can have.

David Knott, Director - Office for Civil Society

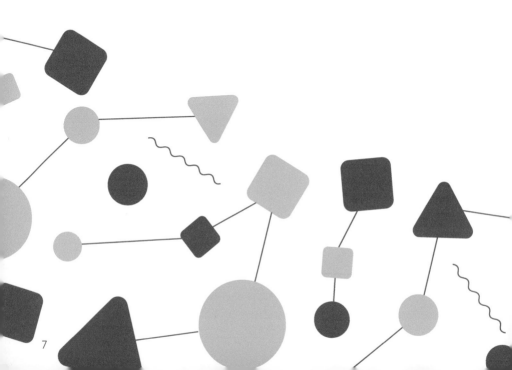

"

The development of the community organising framework two years ago, firmly put power at the centre of our work. This book takes that explanation forward to succinctly explain what organising is and how it can have positive impact on our lives and our communities.

In a world where people are fearful of power and union, we can demystify "power" as simply the power to act and "union" as allyship. This book can give people the space to think about power and privilege in their circles, and how it influences how we behave. It helps us move away from seeing people as service users who need to be fixed to supporting people to become experts who understand their own stories and can bring about the change they want to see in the world. I would encourage anyone to suspend any preconceived ideas about community, read this book and consider how an organising approach can be a shift away from more prescriptive methods of engagement.

Nicola Wallace Dean - Community Organiser
Starting Point Community Learning Partnership - Stockport

INTRODUCTION

This short book is designed to introduce community organising to anyone that has never experienced it before. On **page 15** we define community organising and from **page 16 to 32** we describe community organising through the Community Organising Framework developed by our network, based on ten years or more experience of practising, experimenting with and reflecting on the practice of community organising. On **page 34** we briefly describe some of the different approaches and models of community organising to be found in the UK and internationally.

On **page 38** we then start to look at the many other types of methods and approaches to building community, empowering individuals and taking action for social justice which can be found in use in England today. We briefly look at what they are and then we explain how we see them in relation to community organising - looking at what they have in common and how they differ.

Page 76 contains a summary of the main similarities and common values that we found.

Page 77 summarises the distinctive or defining characteristics of community organising.

_____

This book is not a how-to-guide or a toolkit for doing community organising. Its aim is to shed light on why we believe that community organising is special and distinct and why it matters today more than ever.

WHAT COMMUNITY ORGANISING IS...

Community organising is the work of bringing people together to take action around their common concerns and overcome social injustice. Community organisers reach out and listen, connect and motivate people to build their collective power to effect change.

Community organising is a tried and tested way of effecting change. Thousands of organisers across the world, including in the UK, have developed the approach which has come to be known as community organising. We build on this history. Our definition and framework is not the only one, but it aims to encompass the range of approaches and methods which are collectively known as community organising.

THE COMMUNITY ORGANISING FRAMEWORK

Our community organising framework provides a map of the process. The process usually starts with reach and listening, and it always aims to build power through action. But it doesn't always follow a neat order. It often involves repeating steps or stages several times. The framework helps to keep us on track and to remind us of the steps we need to take to achieve change for good.

Scan the following QR code to visit our website and download a full poster to learn more:

Scan me

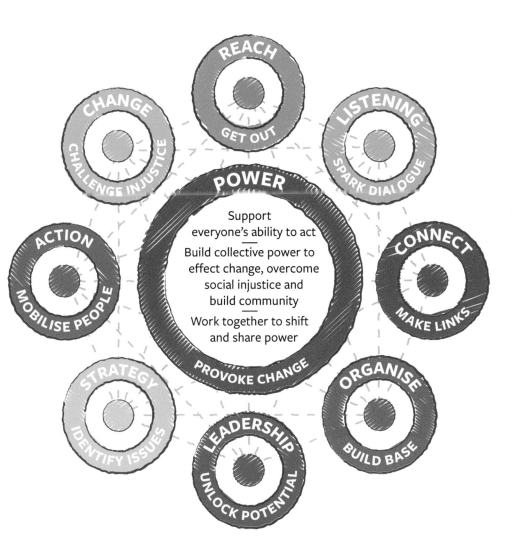

REACH
GET OUT

CHANGE
CHALLENGE INJUSTICE

LISTENING
SPARK DIALOGUE

POWER

Support
everyone's ability to act
—
Build collective power to
effect change, overcome
social injustice and
build community
—
Work together to shift
and share power

PROVOKE CHANGE

ACTION
MOBILISE PEOPLE

CONNECT
MAKE LINKS

STRATEGY
IDENTIFY ISSUES

LEADERSHIP
UNLOCK POTENTIAL

ORGANISE
BUILD BASE

THE FRAMEWORK SECTIONS IN MORE DETAIL

REACH

- Engage everybody and anyone ensuring inclusivity and equality
- Go to where people are

LISTENING

- Develop relationships and identify passion, interests and potential leaders
- Build a picture of people's life in the neighbourhood
- Encourage reflection and explore possibilities
- Challenge people about the way things are

CONNECT

- Connect and create groups of people with shared interests and concerns
- Build bridges between different groups
- Identify community resources, needs and visions
- Share stories

ORGANISE

- Build local democratic and accountable associations of people that can start to act co-operatively and collectively
- Build your power base
- Build a structure

LEADERSHIP

- Develop a culture of possibility where people believe in their ability to create change
- Motivate and support people to take and share leadership
- Identify natural leaders

STRATEGY

- Use stories and information to identify issues
- Understand power and tactics for shifting it through people taking action together
- Analyse information and agree tactics, targets and allies
- Address root causes of concerns whilst tackling immediate symptoms

ACTION

- Facilitate local, regional and national collective action on the issues that matter most to people
  - DIY Action
  - Campaigns
- Bring together and use resources
- Engage with power-holders

CHANGE

- Fight for sustainable change for good
- Strengthen democracy – government by people
- Change hearts, minds and systems to address the root causes of injustice and inequality

POWER

- Support everyone's ability to act
- Work together to shift and share power
- Build collective power to effect change, overcome social injustice and build community

REACH

It's often hard to know where to start when you want to get people to join you in action. But we always start the same way. With reaching out.

We may start with our friends, our families, our neighbours, our members, the people we work with or for. But then we need to go beyond the people we know. We reach out to people we never meet or talk to, through knocking on their doors, standing at school gates, going into community centres, visiting mosques and churches and working men's clubs. We don't believe anyone is hard to reach. We just need to go to where people are. We believe that everyone has something to offer and everyone is a potential leader. We believe it's only through reaching out that we engage people that wouldn't normally get involved in democracy, community or action.

LISTEN

You may have a clear idea about what's wrong and what needs to change, but do others see things the same way? Community organising always starts with face-to-face conversations. The conversations aren't just chats. They are about really listening to what people feel and think.

We listen for three things. What do people really care about? What do people want to do about it? Are they someone who is prepared to get involved? When we listen, we make a connection and we start to build a community. We find the people in our community that can lead us to others, that can unlock doors and help us gain trust. Through listening we build trust.

Listening is not consultation, but it does give us valuable insight into our community. We find out about what is really going on beneath the surface. We hear powerful stories of people's lives. We find out what people love about where they live and what they are angry about. We uncover real problems that need addressing and explore the possibilities for change. We find the assets and resources that a community can build on. We find leaders and we challenge people to act.

CONNECT

As we listen, we start to connect people together. We want people to start to listen to each other and so we create opportunities for that to happen. We invite people to meet up in small groups to talk about the things that matter to them. We ask them to tell their stories. We connect them through what they love, what they care about and what they want to change.

When people start to connect in this way they begin to come up with their own ideas for change. We don't just work with small groups though. We start to link up the groups and to bring them together, breaking down barriers and building bridges. We help people to have good conversations in which everyone has a chance to speak, to tell their stories and to put forward their ideas. We can't agree on everything. So, we look for what we can agree on and what we can work on together to create change for good.

ORGANISE

To really make change takes persistence and power. We may not have a lot of money or political power, but what we have is our people power. If enough people come together, we can change anything, but we need to be organised and to work together well. We also need to know what talents and skills lie dormant in our community and what resources are there to be mobilised.

We believe in democracy and in sharing power and that means we work together in ways that are democratic and cooperative. We keep listening and reaching out and connecting with people until we have enough power to make a change. We call this 'building our base'. When our member base is strong, we can really push for change through the people power of large numbers. We can get things done ourselves that need doing. We can challenge vested interests and unjust power.

LEADERSHIP

In community organising we believe in sharing power. We don't rely on a few strong individuals to lead. We want to give everyone a chance to be a leader. We look for the people that get things done in our communities, that have ideas, that other people look up to, and those that have the potential to do so. We take time to train and develop people, so they can take on different tasks and roles and we give people opportunities to shine.

Shared leadership places less burden on a few individuals. It is more democratic, and it helps us grow our organisation without there being a big gap between leaders and followers. So, we always build a leadership team who work with the community organisers to make plans, to stay in touch with members and to lead action.

STRATEGY ....

To inspire change we need to understand what stands in the way. We need to see where the power lies to prevent or help make a change. This may be political power, or it might be individual behaviour, or it might be the power of money. We take the time to research the problem or injustice we want to tackle. We gather evidence, stories and solutions.

We learn about who stands to gain and who stands to lose from the change we want. We find our allies and we identify who we need to campaign against or whose decisions we need to influence. Or we work out what we can do ourselves to make a change and where we can get the resources we need, to build something better. Often the skills and knowledge already lie within our own community just waiting to be unlocked. Often people are just waiting to be asked.

ACTION

To create change takes action. We will need to use the people power we have built to make action successful. We will need to call on our members to stand up for what they believe in. We will need our community to come together and to commit some time and resources, and sometimes to take some risks. We will need to work together.

Actions may be small, or they may be really ambitious. Action is always non-violent and may require different tactics - such as petitions, events, creative protest, takeovers or boycotts or simply getting on with it ourselves. We might start to clean up our street together or hold a community event. We might challenge a decision made by politicians or campaign to save or develop a service or a resource. We might use our rights to take control of a building for our community. We might mobilise to end an unjust business practice. We might fight to take over a service from the Council because we know we can run it better ourselves. Whatever we do, we will learn from what happened – success or failure – and do better next time.

CHANGE

The purpose of community organising is to win justice, strengthen democracy and build resilient and compassionate communities. Small changes can happen quickly if there are the right conditions and enough energy to create change. It's easier to create change when it involves people coming together to do something themselves - like a clean-up or a timebank or a community coffee morning to tackle loneliness. It's harder when it involves challenging a powerful or bureaucratic organisation or a culture.

We are often trying to change systems and hearts and minds. This can take a long time. Think about how long it took to overcome apartheid, to gain the vote for all adults or to gain civil rights in the USA. Think about how long it took to make drink-driving unacceptable and to bring about gay rights.

We often have to settle for less than we want. We often have to aim for short-term wins on the road to a real and lasting change in power and justice for our communities. In community organising we need to celebrate our achievements and take care of ourselves and our members. Community organising is tiring, and we have to avoid burnout. This is why we keep training new organisers and leaders. This is why it is vital to be part of a movement and care for each other.

POWER

At the root of community organising is a deep understanding of power. We are in the business of building and shifting power. Power is the ability to act and to have control over our lives. Community organising provides the means to act for individuals and communities who feel powerless. We are learning what it means to be powerful together, to act in solidarity with each other. This is the way that inequality and injustice has always been overcome. This is the way democracy works. This is the way community is built. This is the way change happens.

Understanding where power lies is key to building it and redistributing it. We need to be able to see who holds power and this is not always visible. Power is not limited - building our own power doesn't always diminish the power of others. But sometimes power is concentrated in the hands of a few and used unjustly and we need to challenge and change this. We must always use our own power responsibly and for the good of the whole community and especially those with least control over their lives and the least voice in society. Once we have built power, we must constantly ask ourselves if we are using it justly and who is still left out.

Community organising is ultimately a process of creating a more democratic society. It uses approaches which enable people to host good conversations about what matters to them in their community and to decide together how to improve their lives and the world. It encourages people to take part in decision-making. It builds trust between people and politicians. It is a means for people to hold power to account and speak truth to power.

"

Attempting to liberate the
oppressed without their
reflective participation in the
act of liberation is to treat
them as objects that must be
saved from a burning building.

Paulo Freire

OUR PRINCIPLES OF PRACTICE

Our Principles of Practice have been developed to guide all those involved with community organising, to ensure we uphold high standards and act with integrity towards the people we work with.

Scan the following QR code and visit our website to download a full poster:

Scan me

Help people to develop their collective power to act together for the common good of the whole community.

Build on what already exists if that is what the community needs and wants, and co-operate with others.

Put the wellbeing, development and progress of people first.

Take responsibility for maintaining the quality and ethos of community organising.

Work for a just society.

Demonstrate honesty and integrity and uphold public trust and confidence.

Demonstrate respect for diversity and promote equality.

Do not do for others what they can do for themselves.

Manage conflict constructively and non-violently.

Remain Politically neutral.

Do not put yourself or others in danger.

Do not promise what you cannot deliver.

Use the community's starting point as your own, and move at their pace according to need.

NOTES

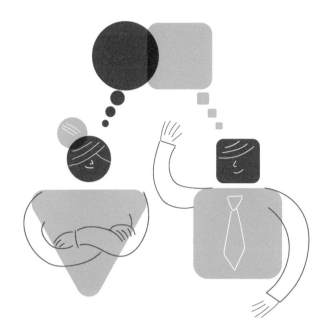

DIFFERENT APPROACHES TO COMMUNITY ORGANISING

Community organising is a distinct set of principles and methods which differentiate it from other forms of community practice, as we discuss in this document.

However, it is also important to say that as community organising has developed across the globe and through time, influenced by some key thinkers and many practitioners, a number of distinctive approaches have developed. We believe that our community organising framework would be applicable to all of these and that all would have similar principles and values to our own. We cannot in this document go into detail about the different approaches, but we should mention a few of the distinguishing characteristics:

Grassroots or neighbourhood-organising starts with individuals recruited on the doorstep or in community settings and gradually brought together in fairly informal networks or tighter structures to take collective action. This is the primary approach which members of the Community Organisers network and our Social Action Hubs use.[i]

Broad-based organising and faith-based organising start with alliances of institutions and listening and action are carried out with and by the members of those institutions. Institutions pay dues to be members of the alliance. The primary proponents of this model in the UK are TCC (Trefnu Cymunedol Cymru / Together Creating Communities) in Wales [ii] and Citizens UK.[iii]

Community or Tenants Unions are a member and dues-paying model of organising, modelled on the Trades Unions and some US based organising groups. Individuals are recruited and signed up as members and are expected to pay a monthly contribution which sustains the organiser. Members run their own branches and plan and take action. In the UK, ACORN [iv] is the main proponent of the model.

Asset based approaches to organising are mostly concerned with building community resilience and self-help. One-to-one listening is supplemented with other types of mapping to build a picture of the resources of the neighbourhood or community and to connect people through their gifts and talents and what they love. This is about building 'power within' individuals and the community. This approach is mostly known as ABCD in the UK and is promoted primarily by Nurture Development.[v]

'Alinsky' or conflict approaches to organising are concerned with building the power of citizens to challenge entrenched or vested power and hold power to account, to win social justice. It is about building 'power with' where people are stronger and act in solidarity together through collective action. Action is used to build people's confidence and leadership and to test the strength of the resistance to change.[vi]

'Freirean' approaches to organising focus on the importance of listening and the way that people come to recognise their own situation in the world, and how they can change it, through dialogue and participatory research, inspired by the work of Paulo Freire.[vii] Organisers using this approach spend a lot of time listening to people individually and building trust and relationships, as well as working with groups to help them analyse their situation using 'codes' which help them develop a strategy for change. This approach was developed as Training for Transformation [viii] in South Africa and adopted by Partners [ix] in Ireland and Action to Regenerate Community Trust in the UK (now no longer operating).

The Organisation Workshop (OW) [x] is an intensive experiential learning experience whereby people develop their understanding of how to organise in large groups. It is usually used to address economic inequalities or issues in a community and can result in the setting up of new cooperative or community enterprises. Organisers act as facilitators and, following an initial listening campaign to identify issues and people, the OW process compresses the organise, leadership, strategy and action phases of the organising framework in one intensive full-time process over a few weeks. So far in the UK, the Organisation Workshop has been run by Marsh Farm Outreach in Luton and Heart of Hastings Community Land Trust.

Identity-based organising is organising around distinct identities such as race, sexuality or age. It arises from direct and structural discrimination and the aim is to reduce inequality and injustices based on these identities. Examples include the civil rights movement, the disability rights movement and the transgender rights movement. Alongside these movements comes the idea of solidarity and allyship - which is where people stand up for others who face discrimination or oppression due to their identity. Recognising and acknowledging privilege due to identity is a key part of allyship and essential for solidarity.

Economic organising is not a well used term but it certainly exists. Think of people organising to bulk buy food, build a community business, create a credit union, start a local produce market or develop a local broadband service. The idea of the 'solidarity economy' is growing stronger - an economy with social justice, cooperation and sustainability at its heart. This approach to organising is allied to the cooperative movement.

"

Those who profess to favour
freedom and yet deprecate
agitation, are men who want
crops without plowing up
the ground. They want rain
without thunder and lightning.
They want the ocean without
the awful roar of its many
waters. Power concedes
nothing without demand. It
never did and it never will.

Frederick Douglass

HOW COMMUNITY ORGANISING RELATES TO OTHER FORMS OF EMPOWERMENT AND SOCIAL ACTION

There are many ways of working with people in communities to create change. These have various aims – such as building community, empowering people, encouraging voluntary action, helping people help themselves and addressing the root causes of disadvantage. But the range of community practices and forms of action can be confusing.

So, what is different about community organising and how does it relate to other approaches?

In this section, we look at how community organising relates to some of the other main social change approaches and forms of action which it may on the face of it resemble. We do not provide a complete guide to each approach. Nor are we critical of any of the approaches discussed here. They all have a part to play. Most are based on some similar values and principles and some share some tools and practices with community organising.

They may be complementary or provide the groundwork on which community organising can build. In some situations, community organising provides the best or only approach to building community resilience or winning social justice for people with little institutional or positional power in society.

We aim simply to explain the basics of each approach or form of action and explain how it relates to or differs from community organising. They are:

FORMS OF OUTREACH AND ENGAGEMENT

- Canvassing and Political Organising
- Community Consultation
- Community Outreach and Engagement

DEVELOPMENT AND DIALOGUE APPROACHES

- Asset Based Community Development – (ABCD)
- Art of Hosting
- Community Development
- Capacity Building

TYPES OF ACTION

- Activism, Campaigning, Mobilising and Social Movements
- Social Action
- Volunteering

ORGANISATIONAL DEVELOPMENT

- Community Organisations
- Community Business
- Unions

PUBLIC SERVICE APPROACHES

- Advocacy and Self-advocacy
- Co-Production and Co-design
- Community Navigators and Connectors
- Local Area Coordination
- Social Prescribing

Please see the final page for a summary of similarities and differences.

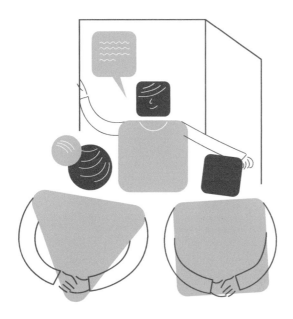

FORMS OF ENGAGEMENT

Community organising is often seen as a form of community engagement, although we would argue that it is much more than that. So, this section looks briefly at some of the different forms of engagement and where community organising sits in relation to them.

CANVASSING AND POLITICAL ORGANISING

Canvassers and political organisers are 'partisan' - loyal to one political Party or platform.

Canvassing is what politicians and Party members do when they knock doors and speak to voters. They aim to understand what issues people care about and what is likely to attract them to their Party. They also try to discover voting intentions and to influence voters, by explaining more about their policies. The purpose can also be to persuade people to turn out to vote on election day.

Political organising, a blend of canvassing, campaigning and community organising, has come to the fore in recent years. It was famously used by Barak Obama in his 2008 election campaign, and more recently in the UK with the setting up of a community organising unit within the Labour Party in 2011 to revitalise the grass-roots of the Party, which has its roots in trades union organising. Movement for Change and later Momentum have deployed political organising tactics in support of the Labour Party. The Green Party has an organising strategy called Target-to-Win. Small and non-mainstream political parties like UKIP depend on organising tactics to break into the political system.

Canvassing is the main tool used by political organisers, along with other tools of organising such as phone-banking and mobilising people around local issues and campaigns - which can then be converted into electoral support. Digital organising using social media has become increasingly important.

There does seem to be an increasing breakdown of the boundary between political and non-partisan organising in recent years. This is because social change usually comes through a mix of political pressure from within and outside the political system.

WHAT'S SIMILAR:

Community organisers and political organisers believe in democracy as the route for achieving social justice and change. They use the tools of door-knocking, listening and building relationships, building power and mobilising people. Many political organisers have trained as non-partisan community organisers and vice versa.

Voter registration and voter turnout are seen as vital in community and political organising. Town hall meetings, candidate hustings and public assemblies are used to mobilise supporters, for political negotiation and to hold politicians to account.

WHAT'S DIFFERENT:

Political organisers have a different goal in building power compared to community organisers. Where community organisers seek to build a non-partisan power base in communities to hold politicians to account, political organisers and canvassers seek to build support and a power base for and through a political Party. Political organisers see the Party as the vehicle for power, rather than a broad-based or grassroots community organisation.

Community organisers do not recommend voting for specific political Parties or candidates - but will analyse the Party or candidate manifestos against the policies they are advocating. Canvassers and political organisers are always partisan.

Political organisers may support community action on issues - as a means of energising supporters and attracting new members - but not as a primary goal.

COMMUNITY CONSULTATION

Community consultation is the process of asking people in a community what their needs are, or what they think about a particular proposal, service or planning issue. It may be carried out by the Council or other public services or by a community organisation. It can be a way of giving people a say in the running of an organisation, the development of a service or the regeneration of a neighbourhood. Sometimes it is a legal requirement.

Often it is done using a survey or questionnaire, but other methods may be used such as focus groups, models and pictures, public meetings or stalls at events, or it can be done through more participatory and deliberative methods such as Citizens Juries, Participatory Appraisal or a Future Search Conference.

Community consultation is primarily about collecting information. Usually the analysis of the information is done by the organisation which is carrying out the consultation. Consultation usually assumes that something is going to be done on behalf of people, not by them, even if it is being done by a community-led organisation.

Sometimes the results are shared with the people who took part. Usually but not always there is no opportunity to get further involved and power remains with those undertaking the consultation. This is different to the best community engagement and to the listening carried out by community organisers through a listening campaign.

COMMUNITY OUTREACH AND ENGAGEMENT

Community engagement means different things to different people and there is no officially recognised definition or approach. Generally, the purpose of engagement is to encourage and maximise people's participation in the development of plans or the design and operation of local services, projects and organisations. However, the purpose and level of participation will vary and can range from consultation on needs to involvement in decision making, through to the community delivering projects and services.

Community engagement activity encompasses a range of approaches and methods and there is strong overlap with other types of activity in this guide - including asset-based community development (ABCD), co-production, art-of-hosting, volunteering etc. Other engagement methods will include participatory research; digital surveys; arts activities; mapping e.g. Planning for Real; forums, assemblies, summits, workshops, conferences and other forms of public meeting; citizens juries; street surveys and door-knocking.

In general, community engagement should be a process of ongoing dialogue between members of the community and the decision-makers or power-holders - rather than a one-off event. It should offer opportunities for influence over decision-making. Some sharing of power should take place but often opportunities to do this are missed.

WHAT'S SIMILAR:

As with community organising, community consultation and engagement involve finding out people's views and opinions through some kind of listening and dialogue process, in order to influence a development, service or organisation.

WHAT'S DIFFERENT:

In community organising, listening has several purposes: to find out what people really care about; to find out what people want to do about it and to find out if they are someone who is prepared to take the lead or get involved in doing something. A listening campaign aims to build a mandate for action.

Community organising is about doing with, not doing for people. Listening in community organising is a dialogue and there is usually no pre-set agenda or pre-set questions. The conversation builds trust and a relationship between the organiser and the person they are listening to. It is the starting point for connecting people up and mobilising them to take action.

Community engagement may go some distance towards sharing power over decisions and resources, however, this is not usually its primary purpose. With community organising, the purpose is to build and shift power over decisions and resources towards a community or group of people that are seeking to win justice or build a stronger community which is better able to care for its members.

DEVELOPMENT AND DIALOGUE

This section looks at practices which, like community organising, emphasise the development of individual and community potential and prioritise dialogue and shared decision-making.

ASSET-BASED COMMUNITY DEVELOPMENT (ABCD)[xi]

ABCD is an approach that originated in the USA, also known as community building. The purpose is 'to build up community groups and voluntary organisations and their informal associations and networks, their collaborative relationships, their shared knowledge and their social power (sometimes called social capital and civil society).' (Kretzman & McKnight 1993) [xii]

John McKnight was a trained community organiser in the Alinsky school of organising. His experience and research on urban neighbourhoods led him to develop an asset-based approach to community organising, focussing on harnessing local resources, capacities and relationships.

The approach starts with mapping and developing an understanding of the positive resources, skills and capacities of residents, community groups and local institutions. Once this has taken place the community builder begins to connect these people and groups together around these assets.[xiii]

The aim is to build pride and confidence within the community. Through focusing on the assets in the community and what residents are already achieving, ABCD aims to build the community's confidence to engage in collaborative relationships with public services, on its own terms, to gain what it needs.

WHAT'S SIMILAR:

ABCD and community organising share many values – not least the belief that communities and people often already have the answers to their own problems and that change must be led by the community itself. Both also focus on the building of relationships and networks. ABCD can be seen as a form of community organising.

WHAT'S DIFFERENT:

Community organising always starts with a listening campaign and building one-to-one relationships rather than mapping assets.

Whilst most community organisers ask about the things that people love and appreciate, we believe it is also important to surface the issues that make people angry and upset. It is often these emotions that move people to take action.

Institutions play different roles. In community building they provide resources. In community organising they are either a way to reach individuals (as in broad-based community organising) - or a holder of power to be held accountable.

Community organising has a strong focus on power, which can be missing from ABCD. It recognises that, to achieve social justice, the collaboration ABCD encourages is not always possible. Sometimes people need to challenge power and provoke conflict to achieve change, especially when resources are limited. Nor do people always feel that they have talents or gifts or a voice to make change or to overcome real barriers such as poverty. They need to develop their confidence and agency through action. Sometimes only system change is the solution and communities cannot be expected to address fundamental injustices through self-reliance and community action alone.

"

At best, we should be locally organized to do both things — advocate and build a neighborhood. The two ways are not in conflict because each addresses a different goal. They are like two different tools. Each is useful but neither can do the job of the other. And the job of a neighborhood organizer is to connect rather than confront, to create rather than demonstrate.

John McKnight

ART OF HOSTING

Art of Hosting is a set of principles and methods for hosting spaces for group conversations and participatory decision-making. Art of Hosting encompasses a varied range of facilitation tools and methods underpinned by principles and ideas drawn from organisational and group theory, social psychology and indigenous or traditional practices such as meditation.[xiv]

The practice involves the design and facilitation of group processes which enable the sharing of power, the managing of complex ideas and diverse opinions, the use of consensus decision-making tools and the sharing of power and leadership within the group. The practice is highly reflective. It has been adopted and used by many sectors - from the corporate world to the environmental movement.

Since 2013 it has begun to be adopted and used in community organising work to enable organisers to host and manage large group processes. These processes really tap into the collective intelligence of the whole community and involve people in decision-making in a way which ensures they are fully committed to action.

WHAT'S SIMILAR:

Community organising and Art of Hosting share values and a core commitment to dialogue and to relational listening. Both draw on the teachings of Paulo Freire and a number of other theoretical and practical roots.

There is a similar commitment to collective decision-making and action and a belief that decisions and solutions come from the people that are involved in or affected by the issue or problem. This results in the conscious planning and design of events and structures that bring people together and enable them to engage in democratic processes and a concern with the development of better organisational forms and structures for decision-making and action.

Supporting new leaders to emerge and to have opportunities to facilitate and lead change is common to both practices.

WHAT'S DIFFERENT:

There is a different understanding of power and how to challenge it in the two practices. Community organising is more concerned with building and challenging the power of vested interests and institutions. Art of Hosting is more concerned with humanising and sharing power by bring people together to have honest conversations and find common ground.

Art of Hosting practice is mostly concerned with seeking common ground and effective solutions through dialogue. It does not always intentionally move people into action after dialogue.

Community organising practice is always about trying to move people into action - individually and collectively.

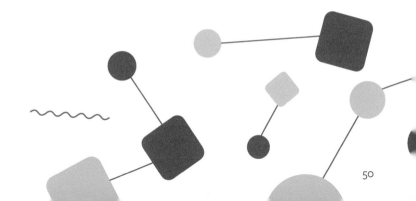

COMMUNITY DEVELOPMENT

Community development has often been used as an umbrella term to cover all forms of community practice including community organising. As such it covers a wide range of community practice with a wide range of aims and may be used in a number of ways. But it is also associated with a professional practice and a set of occupational standards and may be led by qualified professionals working for community organisations and councils.

The National Occupational Standards for community development describe it as a long-term value-based process which aims to address imbalances in power and bring about change founded on social justice, equality and inclusion.[xv] The values that underpin this practice are:

- Social justice and equality
- Anti-discrimination
- Community empowerment
- Collective action
- Working and learning together

Community development (CD) practitioners use a wide range of methods including: supporting informal learning; supporting community activities and events; supporting the start-up of new community or voluntary groups or community enterprises; supporting people to raise funding; supporting people to engage in decision-making processes.

There has been a long debate within the community development field over how far it should seek to become professionalised. However, over the past twenty years or so, some critics argue that is has become increasingly 'top down', especially where practitioners are employed by councils and voluntary organisations[xvi].

WHAT'S SIMILAR:

CD and community organising share values and principles and a focus on the importance of community in people's lives. Both practices share a commitment to justice.

Community organisers and CD practitioners may do many of the same things as part of their practice. Community organisers usually follow a pathway to achieve change which begins with listening and building one-to-one relationships and moves towards powerful collective action. CD practitioners will almost always start by identifying need through some kind of listening or consultation process.

WHAT'S DIFFERENT:

Community development is more likely to be practised by qualified professionals.

Community development practitioners can work with small groups or across whole communities with equal validity - but the goal of community organisers is to build people power and mobilise people to effect change and there is power in numbers.

Community development practitioners are often embedded into public service organisations whereas community organisers prefer to be independent and accountable to citizens directly through a membership or community organisation. Public service organisations can use the principles of organising and support organising in different ways, but need to avoid controlling or directing the process or the outcomes, and to be prepared that they may become the target of an action or a campaign.

A fundamental principle of community organising is that organisers must always be accountable to community members.

The community organising community believes strongly in training and mentoring for organisers but there are not as yet standardised qualifications or routes to becoming an organiser.

CAPACITY BUILDING

Capacity building or capacity development is a widely used term in social and community development but is not always defined the same. Here are two useful definitions:

"Capacity development is the process through which individuals, organisations and societies obtain, strengthen and maintain the capabilities to set and achieve their own development objectives over time. Simply put, if capacity is the means to plan and achieve, then capacity development describes the ways to those means." (UNDP) [xvii]

"When communities come together to form groups and networks, they bring with them a wide range of experiences, knowledge, skills and resources, which help them to address their shared issues and concerns. The extent to which they can do this is called community capacity. Many communities, particularly those which face disadvantage, look for support to help increase their capacity, to help build on or share their existing skills and confidence. The aim is to become more influential to deliver change. This support is called community capacity building." (Scottish Community Development Centre) [xviii]

In relation to communities, we can say that capacity building is the process of developing the skills, resources and knowledge of individuals and community groups in a community, to enable the community to better function, be able to support its members and to achieve positive change.

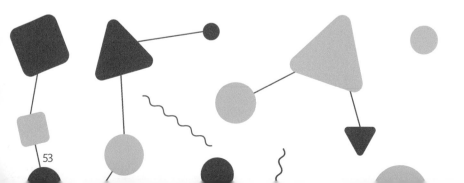

WHAT'S SIMILAR:

Community organisers aim to develop the resources of people they work with, particularly their leadership skills. The aim of a community organising process is to enable a community to plan and achieve change and address their shared issues and concerns. Through taking part in a community organising processes, individuals gain skills and confidence and develop agency.

WHAT'S DIFFERENT:

Capacity building processes may overlook the reality of power differentials and that improving individual skills and knowledge may not be enough to bring change or development to a community. If the law or economic system is unjust or power is concentrated in few hands or there is social inequality, capacity-building may not be enough. Collective action may be more important than knowledge or skills in building confidence and effecting change.

> **"**
> If people don't think they have the power to solve their problems, they won't even think about how to solve them.
>
> Saul Alinsky

ACTION

In this section, we describe a range of forms of voluntary action to sustain community or achieve social change. Community organising always builds towards action, but action may also be sparked spontaneously or as a result of a campaign, a community initiative or individual activism.

ACTIVISM, CAMPAIGNING, MOBILISING AND SOCIAL MOVEMENTS

Activism, campaigning and mobilising are all forms of action to achieve social change.

Activism is usually understood as taking some kind of action to try to make changes in society. There is a huge range of types of activism, including legal, illegal, individual and collective. Activism is often spontaneous but can also be part of a planned campaign. Activism may be individual or collective. Activists are often perceived as lone campaigners - trying to draw attention to a cause which they feel personally committed to, and their actions may be highly visible and involve some risk- such as hunger strikes, sit-ins, citizens arrests or at the extreme end - self-immolation.

Campaigning and mobilising involve picking a target for change – a law, a system or a cultural behaviour – and working to gain the support of allies and to change the minds of opponents to achieve that change. The aim is usually to engage large numbers of people in lobbying, petitioning, demonstrating or taking other forms of direct action for the cause. Sometimes these people are members of the campaign, but others may simply be mobilised through a public callout.

These approaches may be associated with a wider social movement. Social movements tend to be very loosely structured, involving a lot of different groups and organisations who come together occasionally when their interests coincide. They rely a lot on education and public communication methods and increasingly on the use of social media. Some are long-term, but they can also be very short term, arising to drive through a particular change, for example a regime change or a change in the law, and then disappearing once they have won their goal.

WHAT'S SIMILAR:

Activism, campaigning, mobilising and social movements certainly have a close relationship to community organising and community organisers can employ the mobilising tactics and types of action that campaigns and social movements use.

Community organising is a strategy to achieve social change, and these are all forms of action to achieve social change through direct action.

WHAT'S DIFFERENT:

Community organising as a strategy usually sees itself as operating within a democratic context - enabling citizens to engage more effectively in influencing and implementing decisions and intending to make democracy work better for its citizens.

The forms of action discussed above may be used within a range of political contexts including dictatorships and weak democracies - where there is no opportunity to hold politicians to account and the goal is to change the whole system rather than work within it.

Community organising depends on systematic attempts to listen and build the relationships on which long-term change depends and to develop grass-roots leadership i.e. the listen, reach, connect and organise elements of community organising. With activism, campaigning and mobilising there may only be a weak relationship between leaders and those who take part. There may be no ongoing relationship and there may be little or no structure or democratic accountability back to the activists or participants in the campaign. These approaches may become over-reliant on a few charismatic leaders, causing issues with succession and with burnout.

Campaigning and mobilising are often part of a community organising process, at the point when the issues have been identified, power has been built and turnout of people is needed for action to provoke or inspire a change, as in the later stages of our community organising framework. But what community organising offers beyond this is a systematic attempt to build a structure which is strong enough to maintain the commitment of its members, and to support them - both to take action and to sustain the energy needed to drive real change over a longer period of time. It aims to build leadership and accountability between the leadership and members or participants. As such it aims to build a strong and sustainable foundation on which campaigns and activism can build and draw strength. This takes time.

Community organising is not always enough on its own - a combination of structure-based organising (e.g. unions and community unions) and large-scale social movements may be needed to drive change, especially when there is a really big power imbalance and there are entrenched interests to overcome.

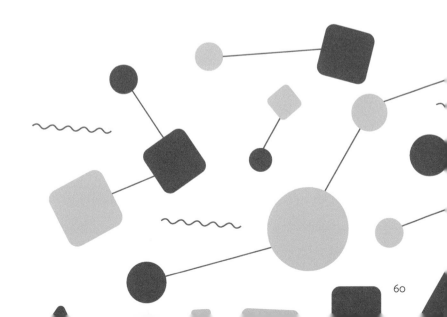

SOCIAL ACTION

Social action is a term that has become well-used in recent years to describe a range of types of activity which sustain society. There are many and varied definitions and descriptions of social action, ranging from that adopted by the Government and mainstream youth sector and others which are more like community organising.

The definition of social action used by Government and the mainstream voluntary sector includes volunteering and charitable giving within social action:

"Social action is about people coming together to help improve their lives and solve the problems that are important in their communities. It can include volunteering, giving money, community action or simple neighbourly acts." [xix]

At Community Organisers, we have adopted a different definition of social action, which is closer to our values and mission. For us, social action is:

"People working together to better people's well-being, strengthen democracy and encourage community life and commitment to others. Social action involves building the power of people working together, taking collective action and achieving a just and caring society."

WHAT'S SIMILAR:

No matter whose definition we are using, social action is about voluntary action by people to improve communities and lives. It is not about statutory services or government action.

WHAT'S DIFFERENT:

Social action, however important it is to the people involved, does not necessarily seek to change an unsatisfactory status quo or address the root causes of social injustice. Nor is it always about collective action or about shifting power. According to the official Government definition, social action can encompass individual charitable giving or acts of service, as well as collective action.

Community organising always involves collective action and seeks a redistribution of power.

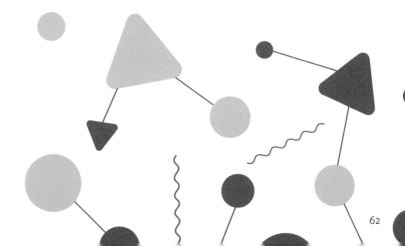

VOLUNTEERING

The National Council for Voluntary Organisations (NCVO) defines volunteering as "someone spending time, unpaid, doing something that aims to benefit the environment or someone who they're not closely related to. Volunteering must be a choice freely made by each individual." [xxi]

This can include formal activity undertaken through public, private and voluntary organisations as well as informal community participation and social action. The most informal volunteering - which we might call neighbourliness - is the glue which keeps communities together, supports families and helps people cope with unexpected setbacks or difficult situations.

Volunteering is important in society and complements essential government services. It is often also needed due to social injustices or failures in community or government that exist. For example, people volunteer in food banks because some people do not have enough money to feed their families. People volunteer in hospitals because we cannot properly fund health services. People volunteer as counsellors due to the high levels of depression in society, which are partly a result of inequality and the lack of adequate mental health services. People fundraise for services which could be funded by the state, such as hospices.

WHAT'S SIMILAR:

Most people who get involved in community organising are volunteering their time. The only exception to this is where there is a paid community organiser.

Volunteering helps to sustain communities - and building strong communities is a key goal of community organising.

WHAT'S DIFFERENT:

We do not usually think of community organising as volunteering. Volunteering is usually associated with doing something for others. But in community organising we are usually involved for our own mutual self-interest. We are trying to change something together that we care deeply about as individuals and as a community. We are engaged as citizens in democracy and community self-help.

The purpose of community organising is to challenge social injustices so that less volunteering is necessary. Community organising seeks to effect change so that society works better for everyone and less help is needed, because there are fewer people in crisis and despair. We seek to get everyone more active in building community and we need to tackle root causes such as poverty, poor housing and health inequalities.

We know that a caring, resilient community requires everyone to give a little time to community activities, to be neighbourly and to be an active citizen, picking up litter and keeping an eye out for children and vulnerable people in our community. There will never be a time when volunteering isn't needed. But as community organisers our purpose is healing society, not just putting a sticking plaster over its wounds.

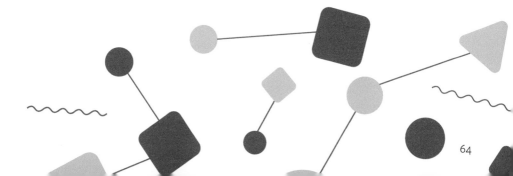

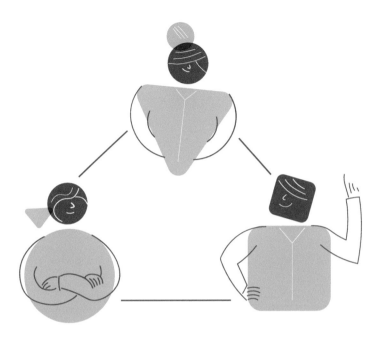

ORGANISATIONAL DEVELOPMENT

Community organising is sometimes confused with the development of community organisations. But the development of community organisations is distinct from community organising in purpose and end product - even though there may be some overlaps.

Community organising as a process requires an organisational structure to support action. Whilst a community-led organisation may be one outcome of a community organising process, they are not the same thing.

In this section we look at the kinds of organisation that may be developed - either through a community organising process or through another kind of development process.

There may be different motivations for setting up a community-led organisation. And there are many different forms and types of organisations. These are a few of the main types which might be the vehicle for a community to support itself - providing services, generating income, owning assets or supporting people - for example. Alternatively, the organisation might only be the vehicle for community organising and nothing else.

COMMUNITY NETWORKS

Community networks are the most informal forms of organisation that can develop. They involve people being connected together, through face-to-face and digital means. There are usually very simple membership criteria with little 'gatekeeping' to enable people to join and leave - for example through joining a Facebook group or attending a social event. Decisions are usually made by those who show up - without much formal democracy. Leadership is often also determined by who volunteers to take on whatever tasks are needed. Networks are usually strongest when they are about communication and engagement and peer support. They are weakest when attempting to organise money, power and collective action.

COMMUNITY ORGANISATIONS

Community organisations are usually legal bodies which are owned or accountable to a specific community (locality or community of interest) through which the members can take certain kinds of action which they couldn't do as individuals. For example, community organisations are often formed to manage a building, give out grants, provide a service or represent the opinion of the community in a decision-making process.

There are a number of different legal forms that a community organisation can take, depending on the degree of formality needed, the type of membership or accountability wanted and the form of funding the organisation relies on. Community organisations usually have some kind of governance structure – a committee, a Board or a leadership team who make decisions. They are often, but not always, charities. To be a genuine community organisation, community members should have the opportunity to take part in governance and influence decisions and direction of the organisation. The simplest type of organisation is a community association - a constituted association with a set of rules and a membership criteria. This is the structure of our local Organising Groups.

MULTI-PURPOSE COMMUNITY ORGANISATIONS

A multi-purpose community organisation serves the whole community and provides a wide range of services and support to meet local needs. These are also known as community anchor organisations, community development trusts or community land trusts.

These types of organisations often own some kind of community centre or hub, which provides a focus for activities or services and a place for the community to come together to learn, celebrate and plan.

Some multi-purpose community organisations deliver services to people in the local community - for example childcare, social care, crisis care. Others run projects which engage people in improving the environment, health, or community development for example.

Some multi-purpose community organisations are engaged in economic development and may own business centres, provide training and deliver contracts or services to generate income. This makes them community businesses as well.

A community land trust often focuses on the development of affordable housing for sale or rent but owned by the community in perpetuity.

COMMUNITY BUSINESS AND CO-OPERATIVES

There are two types of community business: those that generate a profit from selling a product or service which is reinvested into the community; and those that provide a service or product that is directly needed by the community and plugs a gap in the market. Community businesses should always be accountable to the community they serve. [xxii]

Co-operatives are even more accountable. They are democratic business, owned by the workers or the customers, or both.

Owning and operating a community business is a source of power for a community, especially where it is replacing a poor public service or displacing unfair business practices or simply providing for a need which is not met already, such as affordable housing, good food, accessible childcare or a community credit union.

UNIONS

Unions are form of organising in the workplace. "Unions are groups of workers organised together to win a better deal at work. In most workplaces where unions are active, members will get together to talk about what's going on – and any problems they are having. The issues most likely to come up are pay, pensions, safety at work, unfair treatment, or simply the way work is organised." (TUC) [xxiii]

Unions, or Trades Unions, are recognised under law and workers have the right to organise themselves in this way. Unions provide a structure to enable workers to organise to have more power in the workplace and to take action on the issues that concern them. They also have the right to take certain types of action, including to withdraw their labour, or strike. Union history and tactics has been highly influential in the development of community organising. Some community organising approaches are modelled on Unions, for example ACORN describe themselves as "a community based union of working class people – tenants, workers, residents." (Acorn) [xxiv]

WHAT'S SIMILAR:

Organised people can do more than disorganised people. To do most things requires an element of structure and governance. It is easier to be accountable if you have a clear structure and if people can be members and involved in the governance - even if the structure is very simple.

Community organising enables people to self-organise to be powerful and provoke change. Usually some kind of structure is needed to enable us to act together, to make decisions democratically and to raise funds to pay for the time of an organiser. The structure can be relatively informal in legal terms. It does not need to be registered with Companies House or the Charity Commission, but it should have a set of rules or a constitution which sets out aims and membership criteria and how decisions are made. It may be affiliated to a national network or parent body like a trade union branch.

A community organising process can revitalise an existing community organisation. Running a listening campaign renews relationships and an understanding of the community. It uncovers potential leaders who can help to refresh the governance of the organisation. It can help to catalyse new community activity which takes the burden off the organisation to meet all of the community's needs. Community organising could be especially relevant at two stages in the life of a community organisation or business:

- When creating the organisation, through listening to find out what is needed and what the customer or user base might be for the organisation
- When seeking to engage members, rebuild relationships and accountability, refresh the leadership and recruit new members and volunteers or catalyse new community-led activity.

A community organisation which embraces and embeds community organising will be better informed, better run, more accountable and better able to fulfil its mission. [xxv]

WHAT'S DIFFERENT:

There is a risk that organisations focus too much on their own management and survival. A lot of energy may go into sustaining an organisation, generating income, maintaining buildings and ensuring the organisation runs effectively. Even if an organisation is formed as a result of a large-scale mobilisation or campaign, over time it may become inward-looking and cut off from its roots.

It may not keep listening to its members (if it has any) or its community. The organisation can believe that it will become more powerful if it grows its income or wealth or physical assets or gains bigger contracts or provides more services. More members or engagement with people may be seen as a burden and not an asset as there is a cost to engaging with them. The organisation may become more concerned about its public image than its relationships with its community.

With community organising, the organisation is the vehicle through which people act but it is not the focus. The purpose of the organising is to effect change externally. There is always an imperative to keep listening and to keep expanding the base or membership, because the power in organising comes from the people, not from the organisational resources or reputation. Having a proper mandate is what creates power. Understanding what people care about is what enables people to be mobilised to effect change.

Community organising does not start with a pre-defined outcome like setting up a community business. It requires a real analysis of the issue which has been identified and an assessment of all the possible solutions before deciding on the best way of tackling it. For example:

If lack of decent affordable housing is the issue, the solution might be a campaign for licensing of landlords, or we might set up a community land trust to build affordable houses.

An unfair economy is a source of injustice which might be addressed through community organising. Organising around a lack of job opportunities or poor wages or overpriced goods could result in a campaign for a living wage or the setting up of a cooperative business.

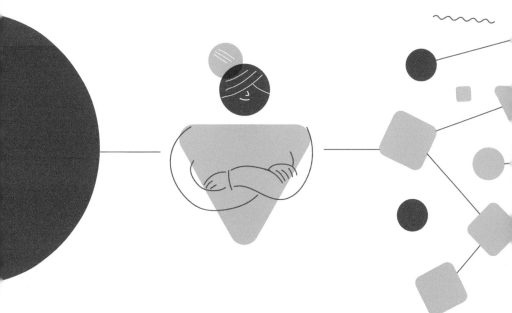

PUBLIC SERVICE APPROACHES

There are a number of approaches that seek to involve
communities more fully and/or make public services more
responsive and accountable, help people to make better use
of public services or avoid using them altogether. This section
explores some of these approaches and how they relate to
community organising. Some form a strong foundation on which
community organising can build. They often employ the ethos
of asset-based community development (ABCD) - building on
people's strengths and loves and their vision for a good life in
their community.

ADVOCACY AND SELF-ADVOCACY

"Advocacy means getting support from another person to help express your views and wishes and help you stand up for your rights. Someone who helps in this way is called an advocate." [xxvi]

"Advocates generally speak for others who are unable to represent their own interests, due to disability, the inherent complexity of the venue such as courts and hospitals, or other factors." [xxvii]

In some circumstances there may be a legal right to have a professional advocate. This is also known as statutory advocacy. Other types of advocacy include peer advocacy, community advocacy and self-advocacy. Advocates may therefore be paid professionals, or they may be volunteers known as citizen advocates.

Self-advocacy is about supporting people to speak up for themselves. Voiceability describe it as follows: "Self-advocacy is about taking control of decisions about yourself and telling others what you want. Lots of people self-advocate every day and take it for granted that they can. The reason why advocacy is so important is that there are thousands of people who aren't able to speak up for themselves. Having an advocate means that there is someone on your side, who will listen to what you want and make sure that your voice is heard. Learning to self-advocate is part of the process. Our aims aren't just to speak up on your behalf; we want you to feel confident enough to tell others what you want." [xxviii]

WHAT'S SIMILAR:

In community organising we also support people to access their rights and to stand up for themselves, but usually through collective action, not individually.

Community organising emphasises the value that is brought by people affected by an issue speaking for themselves and telling their stories. Through listening and one-to-one conversation, we identify the issues that people want to tackle, and we support people to use their voice and their stories to campaign for change.

WHAT'S DIFFERENT:

In community organising we do not aim to advocate for people. The so-called Iron Rule of community organising, usually attributed to one of the founders of modern-day community organising, Saul Alinsky, is "Never, ever do for anybody what he or she can do for themselves". [xxix]

Another way of saying this is the phrase coined by disability rights activists - "Nothing about us without us". [xxx]

A community organising process will aim to gather and mobilise allies from the wider community rather than expecting only those people that are affected by an issue to try to change things. Through the listening and the building of an organising network, people across the community can come together to understand each other better and to create change through solidarity and collective action.

With community organising the aim may be to change a public service or make it more accountable, but it may also be to create alternative models of provision or create community solutions which rely on harnessing the compassion, connections and solidarity of the wider community to improve the lives of vulnerable or excluded people and create a more inclusive society.

"

The greatest lesson of the civil rights movement is that the moment you let others speak for you, you lose.

Ed Roberts

CO-PRODUCTION

Co-production can be described in different ways but is essentially about professionals and citizens – especially users of social and health services - working together to plan and implement a service or a form of support which works better and improves quality of life for people and communities. [xxxi]

There is not one specific way to do co-production. However, it would usually begin with the building of relationships and with facilitated conversations. Usually, but not always, these are done with groups of people rather than one-to-one.

The aim of the conversations would be to understand more about how the current support and services are working and what could be better. They seek to understand people's lives and how services and support could be provided differently and better.

The conversations are not about consultation. People should be involved throughout the process in moving from analysis of the current situation to deciding on and implementing solutions. This is similar to the practise of community organising.

However, co-production conversations usually take place within the constraints of existing resources. The power to make resources available will remain in the hands of professionals and decision-makers.

WHAT'S SIMILAR:

A key value of co-production is that of sharing power between professionals and citizens. In this way it shares an important aim with community organising - the redistribution of power and the transfer of resources from professionals to people.

In both approaches there is a move from consultation and engagement towards people having an equal, more meaningful and more powerful role in services – the planning, development and actual delivery of the service

In both approaches the assets of people who use and provide services - users, carers and staff - are valued and it is recognised that everyone has self-interest, and that this is valid.

WHAT'S DIFFERENT:

In co-production, people and professionals work in equal partnership towards shared goals in service design, but the process is usually initiated by professionals.

In a community organising process, people would move from deciding what is needed to taking action to gain the resources or decisions they need. Using their collective power, they might seek to engage in a process of co-production to design better services. Or instead they might lobby politicians for better welfare benefits or access to employment or for more resources for an existing service. They might campaign for better treatment, or tackle discrimination in access to facilities such as leisure centres, shops or beaches. Or they might set up self-help provision or a community business which meets their needs. Better services are not always the answer.

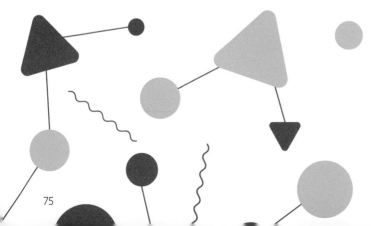

COMMUNITY NAVIGATORS AND CONNECTORS

Community navigators and community connectors are community outreach roles which are found in the health and social care system. They may also be known as link workers or community enablers. The roles and work vary but most are involved in supporting individuals to connect better into the resources available within their community as well as to access statutory health and social care services. [xxxii]

The aim is to take pressure off medical and care services by enabling people to find the support they need within their community and connect with other like minded people, promoting better access to information on local services, groups, clubs and activities.

Navigators and connectors often have specific targets such as working with people aged over 50 or tackling loneliness. They may work with individuals' carers and support networks as well as the individual themself.

Sometimes this is a diagnostic and signposting service, but it may also involve building a longer-term relationship between the worker and the individual.

Additional services which may be offered include:

- One-to-one person-centred service: supporting people and their carers to identify and address barriers to living well and support to navigate systems.

- Support and advocacy services: brokering a range of services to promote independence and pathways to participation in services, e.g. community transport and income maximisation.

- Buddy support: providing support to accompany people and/or their carers to introduce new activities or services if required.

- Volunteering opportunities: recognising older people and their carers as valued assets and helping people find volunteering opportunities.

WHAT'S SIMILAR:

There are a number of shared values and principles, particularly the belief that people can develop their own solutions provided that other people believe in them, and that the solution to people's problems is often not medical or service-based but lies in them finding a place in their community and a network of support.

The asset-based approach to organising is especially similar in that it starts with what people love doing and what their gifts and resources are, rather than with what their problems are.

Another similarity is that these approaches, like community organising, start with a one-to-one conversation which seeks to build a strong relationship between the two people involved. This is the foundation of the future work.

WHAT'S DIFFERENT:

Community organising is concerned with supporting collective action rather than individual needs and we do not signpost people to other services unless we come across a vulnerable person with safeguarding needs.

In community organising we try to see everyone as a citizen and member of the community, not someone in need of services. We aim to help them to tell their story and use their experience to effect change. We believe that everyone has something to offer and seek to work with people at their own pace so that they can become involved in their community and start to become part of collective action.

Sometimes people are not ready for this. They need to take care of their own needs first before they can turn their attention to some kind of community action. So, connectors and navigators could provide a foundation of individual support from which community organising can build.

LOCAL AREA COORDINATION (LAC)

Local Area Coordination is a practice which has come to the UK from Australia in the past 10 years. It is an approach which aims to support people with disabilities, mental health needs and older people (and their families/ carers) to achieve their vision for a good life, to support people to be part of and contribute to their communities and to strengthen the capacity of communities to welcome and include people. [xxxiii]

Individuals self-refer or are found by the coordinators but are usually vulnerable adults in some way or in a phase of their life where they need support outside of their own family resources. Local area coordinators are based in their local communities as a local, accessible, single point of contact for these people and their families. They take time to get to know and build positive, trusting relationships with individuals, families and local communities.

It is in many ways similar to the work of community connectors, navigators and enablers but is usually more long term. Local area coordination also aims to drive reform and systems change across services: making services more personal, local, flexible, accountable and efficient. For example, the process may identify gaps in community opportunities and can then start new partnerships to actively develop local community resources. It supports people to have a voice through supporting self-advocacy, advocating alongside people or advocating for people.

WHAT'S SIMILAR:

Like community organising, Local Area Coordination starts with one-to-one conversations about what a person cares about and what their vision is of a good life in their community. The conversation is about building a trusting relationship. Also, like community organising, the work is about fostering a more compassionate community with stronger bonds which can better support individuals.

SOCIAL PRESCRIBING

Social prescribing is a fairly recent health initiative, which aims to help the number of people who visit GPs over and over with chronic problems or conditions that may have social solutions. [xxxiv]

Social prescribing starts with a conversation with an individual to find out what their interests are. That individual will then receive a community-based prescription, intended to improve health and well-being as an alternative to a medical intervention.

Various things may be prescribed, for example - exercise, a social group, volunteering, an art class, nature or work experience.

In some approaches the social prescribing link worker may simply sign-post the individual to the social or community provision after a one-off interview and move on, whereas in others there is an ongoing relationship for a specific or open-ended period of time. In the latter the social prescribing work is similar to the work of community navigators, connectors and local area coordinators, but is usually based in primary care settings rather than wider health, social care or community settings.

As part of the Long Term Plan published by NHS England in 2019 there is a commitment to having 1,000 social prescribing link workers in place by

2020/21 who will be employed by Primary Care Networks in England. In addition the Government has also committed to establish The National Academy for Social Prescribing. [xxxv]

WHAT'S SIMILAR:

Like community organising, social prescribing starts with a one-to-one conversation with the patient. The aim is to give them more control over their condition and to create the opportunity for real and lasting behaviour change, and to connect them to others who can provide peer support and make them feel part of a community.

WHAT'S DIFFERENT:

Social prescribing usually results in a person being sign-posted to a community activity or group. Sometimes there is ongoing support and coaching to encourage the person to take up the prescription. Patients are only treated as individuals who need to change their behaviour, not citizens who may also need to change society.

The options available to social prescribing depend on the resources available in the community. Patients are not usually supported to develop new community activities which meet their needs or to start a campaign to change social conditions or services.

Community organising by contrast does lead to new community groups and projects. By fostering collective action for social change, community organising can support social prescribing by ensuring that the community has the resources on which social prescribing and its patients can draw. It can connect patients up with others who feel as they do. It can help them to organise themselves to tackle the cause of their condition or to have a voice in the health service. It can also provide the potential for a more holistic approach, by giving them the opportunity to engage as full citizens in their community.

NOTES

WHAT ARE THE MAIN SIMILARITIES BETWEEN COMMUNITY ORGANISING AND OTHER APPROACHES?

People-centred	Redistributing power from government or public services to people	Listen to people and understand their interests, motivation and aspirations	Seek ways for people to be more active, engaged, and to participate
Commitment to civil/human rights and social justice	Work towards more caring, supportive communities	Encourage people to speak out and have a voice	Encourage self-help and self-development
Build people's confidence and recognise what they have to offer society	Believe in an ideal of social good, collective good, or a good life	Participation is voluntary and valued	Solutions are within individuals and/or communities
Believe in the possibility of positive change - hopeful	Seek to unlock people's talents and capacities	Create connections and relationships which strengthen community or institutions	Value diversity and promote equality

HOW TO RECOGNISE COMMUNITY ORGANISING

Not all of these features are present in every community organising process or practice. But these are the features which we believe are most essential to a community organising process, and without which we would need to ask the question - is this really community organising?

Community organiser is accountable first and foremost to the members and to the community

Members pay towards the cost of the organising where possible to maintain autonomy

Always begins with a listening campaign - sometimes, but not always, with door-knocking

Building strong, trusting relationships with members and leaders through 1-to-1 conversations

Organisers connect people together around their interests and build alliances

People tell their stories and use their personal experiences as a tool for change

The agenda and solutions come from the people, not from politicians, funders or organisations

There is explicit commitment to build, challenge and share power with and for those who have none.

Organisers mobilise people to build a power base for change and to create new power relationships

Action is part of the strategy for change – action can be a tactic or a goal in itself.

The organiser doesn't do for people what they can do for themselves

Organising challenges people to be part of the solution and not just blame others for what is wrong

Teaching leadership and training leaders and members in how to organise is integral

Organising seeks to strengthen democracy not replace it, avoid it or work around it

There is commitment to winning justice and building community through collective action

The action-reflection cycle is essential to the process

REFERENCES

i. https://www.corganisers.org.uk

ii. https://www.tcc-wales.org.uk

iii. https://www.citizensuk.org

iv. https://acorntheunion.org.uk

v. https://www.nurturedevelopment.org

vi. http://industrialareasfoundation.org

vii. https://www.freire.org

viii. http://www.trainingfortransformation.co.za

ix. http://www.trainingfortransformation.ie/index.php/what-we-do/courses/training-for-transformation

x. https://en.wikipedia.org/wiki/Organization_workshop

xi. https://www.abundantcommunity.com/home/authors/parms/1/which/john_mcknight.html

xii. https://resources.depaul.edu/abcd-institute/publications/Documents/GreenBookIntro%202018.pdf

xiii. https://www.scie.org.uk/publications/windowsofopportunity/localassets/assetbasedworking.asp

xiv. http://www.artofhosting.org

xv. http://cldstandardscouncil.org.uk/resources/standards-and-benchmarks/national-occupational-standards/

xvi. Ledwith, Margaret (2011) 'Community development: A Critical Approach, 2nd Edition' (BASW/Policy Press Titles) ISBN 978-1847426468

xvii. https://www.undp.org/content/dam/aplaws/publication/en/publications/capacity-development/capacity-development-a-undp-primer/CDG_PrimerReport_final_web.pdf

xviii. https://www.scdc.org.uk/hub/community-capacity-building/more

xix.   https://www.gov.uk/government/publications/centre-for-social-action/centre-for-social-action

xx.   https://www.corganisers.org.uk/training/become-a-social-action-hub/

xxi.   https://www.ncvo.org.uk/ncvo-volunteering

xxii.   https://www.powertochange.org.uk/what-is-community-business/

xxiii.   https://www.tuc.org.uk

xxiv.   https://www.acorntheunion.org.uk

xxv.   https://www.corganisers.org.uk/news-blog/social-action-hub-framework/

xxvi.   https://www.mind.org.uk/information-support/guides-to-support-and-services/advocacy/

xxvii.   Schutz, Aaron. "Core Dilemmas of Organizing: What is Community Organizing? What isn't Community Organizing?" www.educationaction.org/

xxviii. https://www.voiceability.org/about-advocacy/self-advocacy/

xxix.   Chambers, Edward T (2003) , Roots for Radicals: Organizing for Power, Action, and Justice (Continuum International Publishing Group. ISBN 0-8264-1499-0.

xxx.   Charlton, James I (1998) 'Nothing About Us Without Us' University of California Press. ISBN 0-520-22481-7.

xxxi.   https://www.scie.org.uk/publications/guides/guide51/what-is-coproduction/defining-coproduction.asp

xxxii.   https://www.hee.nhs.uk/sites/default/files/documents/Care%20Navigation%20Competency%20Framework_Final.pdf

xxxiii. https://lacnetwork.org/local-area-coordination/

xxxiv.   https://www.england.nhs.uk/wp-content/uploads/2019/01/social-prescribing-community-based-support-summary-guide.pdf

xxxv.   https://www.gov.uk/government/news/social-prescribing-new-national-academy-set-up

LAST WORDS

This book was inspired by conversations with and stories from our amazing network of experienced community organisers and trainers. In particular I would like to thank Helen Wallis-Dowling, community organiser and training lead at Community Organisers, for all that she has contributed to our understanding of community organising and to our training and education curriculum.

I would like to thank the participants in a session we ran for our trainer network in October 2018 when we started to explore what is unique about community organising and what it shares with other practices – which really led to this guide. I acknowledge the helpful conversations between Nick Gardham and Cormac Russell of Nurture Development about community organising and ABCD. I thank the participants in a workshop that Helen and I ran at our annual event in 2019 on the history and global roots of community organising, and the participants of a Round Table discussion for Public Sector colleagues in January 2019. I thank the members of Imagine, our learning advisors for the Community Organisers Expansion Programme, and especially Marilyn Taylor, who commented on an early draft of this book.

Most of all I acknowledge the work and writings of countless thinkers, listeners, organisers, community workers, campaigners and activists across the world who continue to inspire and teach us. Needless to say, all mistakes or misrepresentations are ours alone.

Naomi Diamond, December 2019

As we publish this book, we know that many people feel alienated from politics and are losing faith in democracy to deliver justice. They are losing heart and losing hope. Communities are without vital support services and the coming climate crisis requires us to come together to resist, adapt and build resilience. There has never been a more important time to listen to each other, to join together, to hold the powerful to account, to care for each other and to support and take action in our communities and lives. We must not be held back by our differences – we must build on our shared values and together transform our country, one community at a time.

Nick Gardham, December 2019

"

To bring about change, you must not be afraid to take the first step. We will fail when we fail to try.

Rosa Parks

ABOUT COMMUNITY ORGANISERS

Community Organisers is the national membership body and training organisation for community organising in England.

Our mission is to ignite social action in communities, embed community organising locally and in different sectors, and develop a strong network and sustainable future for neighbourhood community organising.

We believe in the collective power of people and that when people get together they can create positive change that will transform their neighbourhoods.

Across our networks we are inspiring thousands of people to take action – whether setting up a new community-led housing project, lobbying for better public transport, challenging cuts to health services, or establishing community owned enterprises. These actions, are all contributing to building a powerful movement that is both shifting and sharing power, ensuring those people most distant from decision making can be heard, be powerful and make change for good.

Scan me
TO VISIT OUR WEBSITE

https://www.corganisers.org.uk

National Academy of
Community Organising

THE NATIONAL ACADEMY OF COMMUNITY ORGANISING

The National Academy of Community Organising (NACO) provides quality assured training and Qualification courses in community organising.

The National Academy of Community Organising (NACO) is the training arm of Community Organisers. It is a network of affiliated local hubs of community organising known as Social Action Hubs. These organisations deliver our courses.

There are currently 22 Social Action Hubs across England. They are locally rooted organisations that are committed to community organising and are inspiring the many thousands of people across our network to take action in their communities. They use their experience to support people to develop their understanding and practice of community organising through training, support and mentoring.

Each Social Action Hub is unique and works in its own way to ignite social change through community organising, However, all of the Social Acton Hubs are quality assured by Community Organisers to offer our training courses.

NACO also has a pool of associate trainers who can offer our training in-house or in other areas where there is currently no Social Action Hub.

Scan me
TO VISIT OUR WEBSITE

https://www.corganisers.org.uk/NACO

FINAL REFLECTIONS

PASS IT ON...

Thank you for taking time to read the book.
Now it's your time to take action!

Please feel free to **pass the book on** to someone else who, like you, is keen to learn more about community organising.... or, share something you've learnt with us on one of our social media channels:

@corganisers   @corganisers   facebook.com/
                                              COrganisers

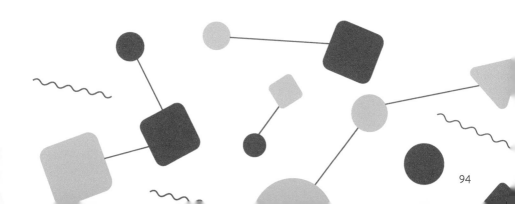

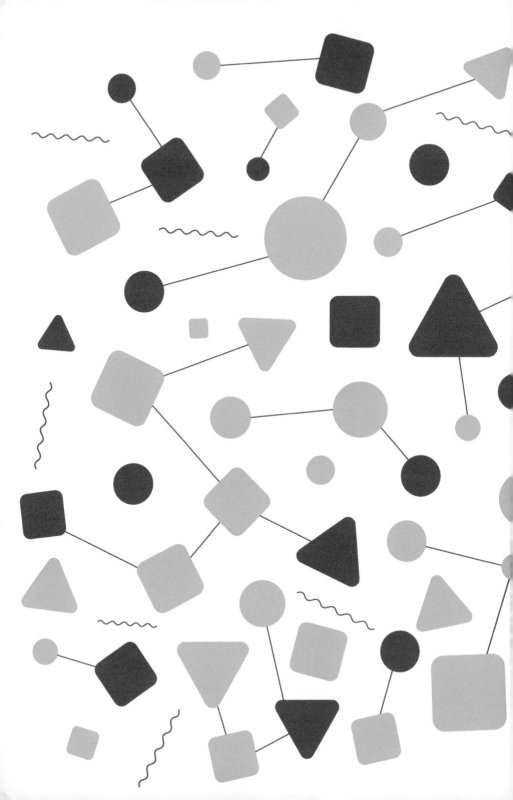